More 1
The Sager Group

MW00380794

See our entire library at TheSagerGroup.net

Students write the Darnedest Things

Gaffes, Goofs, Blunders and Unintended Wisdom from Actual College Papers

Pamela Hill Nettleton, PhD

Illustrations by Kevin Cannon

Students Write the Darnedest Things:

Copyright © 2022 Pamela Hill Nettleton, PhD

Cover and Interior Illustrations by Kevin Cannon
Interior design by Siori Kitajima for PatternBased.com

Cataloging-in-Publication data for this book
is available from the Library of Congress.
ISBN-13:
Paperback: 978-1-950154-92-0
eBook: 978-1-950154-91-3

Published by The Sager Group LLC
TheSagerGroup.net

Students write the Darnedest Things

Gaffes, Goofs, Blunders and Unintended Wisdom from Actual College Papers

Pamela Hill Nettleton, PhD

Illustrations by Kevin Cannon

THE SAGER GROUP

Artifex Te Adiuva

Contents

1

Welcome to Class

I am a college professor.

My classrooms are filled with young people who are leaving their teens and entering their twenties. I like that age of human.

They are feisty and playful, with high energy and big dreams. So much is new to them and they share their wonder and enthusiasm generously with me. I love my students. So when they make egregious writing blunders, I know it's not because they are incompetent or ill-educated.

They do not reread what they write, despite my persistent and charming nagging on this step that every professional writer knows is essential.

They consider revision redundant—once they get words onto the screen, that's good enough, and they are on to the next assignment.

They do too much, juggling five courses with working a part time job, learning how to make mac and cheese, and attempting to solve the mysteries of dorm laundry machines.

And many hail from elementary, middle, and high school systems that nobly emphasized creativity and self-expression over grammar and sentence structure—and these quotes are overflowing with creativity and self-expression.

Over the last few decades, I've had the honor of teaching in several excellent U.S. universities. As I graded, I collected student writing gaffes because they were funny and charming and sometimes even excellent teaching aids to use anonymously in class. Seeing actual mistakes made by their peers far more persuasively galvanized students to reread their sentences and double-check their work than me wagging a grammar book at them ever could.

Each quote in this book is from a real student, submitted for an actual assignment. Most are from my courses, but colleagues teaching at universities and colleges all over the country also sent me gems from their own grading adventures. The punctuation, spelling, grammar, and conceptual errors are intact as I found them.

The majority are quotes from the days before autocorrect, so we can't blame technology for these delights. In recent years, I weeded out quotes that seemed likely to have been caused by an overhelpful app, saving only the kinds of inventive goofiness it takes a human brain running behind deadline and on sheer adrenaline to manufacture—especially when it's trying to be Very Serious and Say Something Pithy.

I didn't shame or name these student writers in class nor do I here—I never attached names to the quotes and I don't remember who wrote what—but I do genuinely thank them for helping us all learn.

The students who made these errors of haste, naivete, inexperience, and—I'll go ahead and say it—the passing cluelessness of youth help us all challenge our assumptions and work to express ourselves more clearly. This book is dedicated to them and to every one of my students.

I am grateful for their winsome examples of how what a writer means to say does not necessarily resemble what lands on the page. Sometimes with a great, big, juicy plop.

—*Pamela Hill Nettleton, PhD*

P.S.

And, lest you think the professor with the red pen wrote a book with a misspelled title, both "darnedest" and "darndest" are acceptable spellings for a word meant to stand in for "damnedest," but with nicer manners. Fans of the version used on this cover include the Oxford Learners Dictionary, the Cambridge Dictionary, the Collins English Dictionary, the Washington Post, The New Yorker—and the Scrabble Dictionary.

Almost the Right Word

Why stop and click on "thesaurus," right there on your keyboard, when you can just keep writing, guess at the spelling, and hope that it probably, more or less, means roughly the right thing?

In this essay, I will spawn and reflect on three key lessons about professional communication.

—Please don't make me watch.

Tears were stinking in her eyes.

—*And screaming down her cheeks.*

I rustled over the idea.

Miss Honey wears a welcoming
pink dress.

With our uniformed passion, our clients will feel seen and heard.

—Especially with those brass buttons.

I am defiantly guilty of doing it.

I excel at outreaching across people.

As we look back on how television has changed, we've gone from having a few channels and networks to having hundreds of channels disposable at our fingertips.

—*Some days, it does feel like that.*

I hope you come to our meeting to help us anatomize this issue.

It is not accepted for women to dress
more proactively.

It is significant to me to reach toward virtuosity consistently. I believe that being virtuous in myself will also benefit those around me.

Lew Wasserman was notorious for supporting the Democratic party.

She gracefully bounces across the entire stage.

The crew was trained and certified, and regally ran evacuation drills.

This interview was impressionable.

I never really watch FOX news but I
can tell that it is very screwed when it
comes to politics.

The taste of the common variety of Brie is typically severed with crackers.

The Ted Talk presenter makes excellent use of humor to hummer her points.

There had been rumors, but until now, everything was based on heresy.

I am analyzing female couches and refs
in the NFL and how they are portrayed
in media.

A successful speech should be contagious.

By the end, the fatigue is infatuating
the air and infecting everyone.

Even though this news outlet is afflicated in many places its central location is in Atlanta.

The second practice that was being
misused was the altercation of the
photographs used in the newspapers.

The stagecoach calls characters and directs them on and offstage.

Her anger and resistance, we find, comes from the amour she has put up following her previous relationships.

I couldn't tell if he was
over exaggerating things or
under exaggerating.

Make yourself extinguishable.

Unlike Newsweek, Time states the number of casualties, honoring the diseased.

Wasserman anticipated the successful perversion that was television.

Waste piles have overflown into
our oceans.

While Johnny is smitten, Frankie is
understandingly cautious, believing it
to be a fling. She is constantly turning
down his filtration.

Yahoo has been accused of imploring a far left-leaning agenda.

Reviving news from journalists is the
main way I intend to diminish the
influence of propaganda and
invention from my life.

Lastly, as discussed in this week's presentation on persuasion, she was able to use strong pervasive techniques.

In this analysis, I will dissect the ethical codes, theories, and principles within the media that swarmed this case.

One thing I learned from your speech was how to give a calm, collective, but still professional delivery.

—*And I wasn't even talking about communism.*

The film "Bonnie and Clyde" was a self-righteous and acoustically dangerous crime against the Great Depression.

Following that, we see Gloria who is clearly from a different country shown by the inaudible accent she has.

They were lying on their sides with
their hands swiftly laid on their
breasts.

3

Stating the Obvious

Some things sound so profound when you write them. Not so much when you read them.

The authors of these two texts are from their own countries.

Authenticity is something that cannot be faked.

Comedy will not be going away any time soon.

Death is something that everyone has
to face at some point in their life.

Development starts young in children.

Every comment under each article
has validity.

Every word comes weighed down with expectations & assumptions of what they mean.

I believe that everything affects us, whether on a conscious or subconscious level.

If we plan to figure out how to stop this
concept, we must learn how to solve
this problem.

It began as a war between two sides.

Many people can agree that intelligence is a common goal and achievement around the world.

Media is a perfect medium to make the voices heard.

Sleeping is internationally universal.

Written communication is very
prevalent in the world today.

Communication is the cornerstone
to any successful conversation
since understanding leads to good
conversation.

This epidemic of doping in cycling has and continues to reinforce the cultural norm of doping in cycling.

History plays its role in writing, scripting, and acting that the history transcript divides us as we learn from the media and history itself.

It's uncomfortable to me to think of a world where we are equal because the world I've been shown, but the future isn't based on the past.

Growing up myself it was difficult to find a character in movies or film that had the same values as myself while still looking and growing up the way I did.

We are all American citizens, except those that aren't citizens of the U.S.

—And now we're back where we started.

4

Everybody's a Critic

Curious things happen when students who may not have been exposed to many cultural events yet—because they haven't been on the planet that long—write reviews of plays, ballet, opera, galleries, and fine dining.

I walked out of the theater indifferent toward my feelings for the film.

The Coq au Vin is visually appealing,
as the sauce is drenched all over the
chicken and potatoes. The red wine-
braised chicken breaks apart easily,
making it easy to eat in minutes. Mixed
with the creamy, garlicy mashed
potatoes, the combination does enough
to make you want to go back. There is
so much flavor, but not to the point that
it is overwhelming. The only thing to
improve it is to pair it with a nice beer
or a rum and coke.

The painting looks like some type of
bomb or missal that, when opened,
small bugs float across the image.

One of the most important aspects of a
ballet is the dancing.

It can be no surprise that the reaction to the film was bittersweetly groundbreaking.

The play Frankie and Johnny attempts to tell a compelling romance story, but lands on the end of misogyny.

—*Ouch.*

From the first dancing sequence in the opera, it is clear that the ballet is void of any kind of dialogue.

Lively, witty, and expressive, this
magical musical clutches the audience's
heartstrings and kills them
with laughter.

Dancers signal to one another in an unconventional splay of birdcalls.

The cast, old and young, performed each song as if they were a competitive cheerleading squad competing for nationals. They were *that* sharp.

—*About an award-winning West End theatre production in London.*

He is shown to be her Romeo, always there to guide her and help her make the "right" decision.

—*After all, that worked out so well for Juliet.*

The two share a dance and within
minutes the show transgresses from
the high-spirited motion of friends to
the fluid movements of lovers.

The scenes bounce around to
different locations.

Three tiny, deep friend balls are in the center of the dish.

—*He means "fried."*

His exhibition has pieces featuring beadwork, weaving, and a sculpture made entirely out of beads of a Native American man.

He masters the art of feminism
excruciatingly well. He struts across
the stage, he crosses his legs when
sitting down, he even has a bit of a
dancing number, causing him to flick
his legs into the air.

—I wonder how he'd play patriarchy.

The musicians are rousing and violent
while still remaining in sync with
one another.

—I think I was at that concert.

Their duets were memorizing.

Her facial acting was dually impressive
all night long.

Singing while gazing into each other's eyes, duets were momentous.

This film has been taught over the years in my schooling years, whereas I grew up to keep learning about things being taught in society that had changed so much when I started to learn something and understand them in a way that will affect me.

The top tier of the pastries is the last
unknown world to unconquer.

Do not be frightened by the word "snail." It is just an insect, and a delicious one at that.

—*Escargot are gastropods, actually.*

We all tried the escargot so nobody had
to be subconscious of slug breath.

One film will never satisfy the ideas
derived from experiences people
have had.

These three matching items are automatically drawn to the viewer's eyes.

When approaching Gibson's work, my
eyes flow through the entire piece.

I think the build-up of this film and
the pressure shows it is really a
trailblazer for representation, which is
unfortunate.

While people do not know what it's like to have consumption or live in a time without indoor plumbing, the audience can relate to falling in love and going broke while young.

5

I Don't Know Where I'm Going—Follow Me!

To write, you need a screen, a keyboard, and a GPS to keep track of your thinking.

The media constructs identities in worm holes. They demand society to fit in these holes and belittle any member who does not. Advertisements in particular use this worm holes to their advantage.

—*I promise, I never lectured on worms or holes.*

I teach media studies.

I believe that individuals in our society base off how they look when they compare themselves to what is being portrayed in the media being shown across all platforms.

Action derives from the initial attempt
we are making, based on decisions that
we deem as most beneficial, which helps
us grow and develop more in society.

I hoped that how ideas were introduced
was much more straightforward than
they were and intended to be grasped in
a pretty big way.

They are master lyricists and woodworkers behind an old-school piece of furniture that when sitting down to listen to it, it sinks, enveloping a sound and mood that make it damn-near impossible to get out of in the best possible way, leaving listeners content and in no rush to leave.

Not simply representation but the way we treat people and how we see them, even if we don't believe the bias, we most likely still have one.

Of course, not everything can be specifics, but when all normalcy falls to the "white males daily lifestyle," it can be hard to compromise.

Going into the ghetto is like following someone on Twitter that is from a small unknown independent magazine about gays or lesbians.

—*Yes. Yes it is. It is exactly like that.*

Racial identity is the segregation behind so much issue in the U.S. because of the White supremacy that happens at the beginning of a history that is marked.

We live in an era where we are scared
to ask the questions that make me
uncomfortable and to have our toes
stepped on when in reality it is the
silence with these tough topics that
create ignorance and ignorance that
leads to chaos.

—*As long as you're not uncomfortable,*
the rest of us will be just fine.

I significantly know that there are generally several ways for most online professors to potentially mostly stop such work or even, for the most part, threaten the learning experience of students, or so they thought.

This identity provides several accounts of elements that create ambivalence in perceiving this identity.

The term was first coined in 1969 and has been around even longer.

It is when there are more definitions
granted from these adaptations in film
that the standard of self that people see
for themselves as no longer abnormal.

Rap artists evolved into the misogynistic lyrics that we see today but that is not what it was built on.

We would certainly not have a good sense of as many cultures as we had today if each culture believed in the same series of values that made each culture special.

The connection between the toxic relationship of women and their bodies in comparison to the outlet of the fashion industries advertising strategy is a parallel example of the power in this realm of media.

The harmful consequences of this stereotype continue to remain in the current bias coming out of the gap of treating reports of people of color in media isolation.

Coming into analyzing mass media sources it was clear that who owned these programs affected everything more negatively but in this case, shapes cultural ideology positively in the same instance.

Taking advantage of the media's reputation by creating fake news holds us back from making any progress to becoming educated when taking part in action.

In societies being able to show the truth and understanding can help create a better more understanding than the untrue things that are displayed about a country that is a beautiful place. Still, within its country, there are a lot of hidden truths.

We are the viewed need to hold accountability for the diversification of the fashion world and the advertising world so they can come together and create realistic, relatable content that may even have the chance to receive even more interaction because people will be able to positively compare.

For example, he did not like the way commercials transitioned from a donate, military requirement and fried chicken call to action.

—*Follow Colonel Sanders unto the breach!*

People may believe that they should be
revealed to the Internet without being
harmed by it, but this seems to be an
unlikely thing to do.

Television has been a friend to me in a number of ways, when you think about your life and situations you've been in you turn to others who have been in the same situation, and sometimes when you're working to figure out life you might turn to sitcoms or shows that allow you to watch someone else navigate a similar situation with some sort of comedic relief, it allows you to feel more comfortable about a life you have not yet lead.

—It's one sentence. Really.

Gender Trouble

When you're just starting to think critically about gender-related attitudes, it's easy to think right and write wrong.

Males, much like females, are a gender.

—This was written by a brilliant graduate

student and I know what he meant.

Gender studies were originally focused

on women, as if that was the only gender.

Unfortunately, rich, white, and heterosexual does not describe 100 percent of the population.

—*Well, we're not all bummed about that.*

Women are often cast as unintelligent characters so for them to carry out the heist plan without screwing up was positive for gender blindness moving forward.

—*We'll take our progress where we can find it.*

Beyond a young man's initial
sexual start-up, men who divulge
in misogynous rap lyrics will more
often contribute to elongated periods
of aggressive and painful behavior
towards their female partner than men
who divulge in non-misogynous lyrics.

We see many women making non-verbal remarks towards Renee's confidence.

—And those hurt the most, really.

Rosalind brings the idea that "inside every woman is a man."

—*And takes it with her when she leaves, hopefully.*

Naturally, media is able to fill this void and provide for us the ideals that we as a society have come to know that put genders in their own boxes with little room for any indifference.

          —As long as we're moving forward.

These misrepresentative images put
negative pressure on women to look
a certain way, when in reality, they
probably look just fine.

—We appreciate your support, fella.

It is unfortunate that women are either seen as horrible, threatening executives or homemakers.

Women have been the target of much
scrutiny throughout the world.

Even though amazing women have come out of the woodwork to gain major acknowledgements within the news industry, women have not gained the full respects that men have within the same positions.

> —*Maybe they should stop crawling out of the baseboards and get proper desks.*

He seemed to bring up positive
representations of women saying,
"show me something natural, like an
ass with some stretch marks."

—*Say, that* is *positive.*

Misrepresentation is commonly found in all types of media, and women have always seemed to be at the forefront of it.

—*Well, at least now we know who to blame.*

Masculinity in American society and television shows strong, hairy men dressing in simplistic outfits and often doing physically demanding tasks like working on a farm or being a cowboy. And of course, being physically attractive with a strong jawline.

Opening the door for a more masculine approach to therapy and headspace by promoting marital arts, for example, is a good start.

—*Get away from me with that downward dog, you cad.*

Male Masculinity is not always talked about or noticed.

—And yet, it's always there, just lurking.

The concept of masculinity has always
been rooted in the fear of acting like
a woman, which depicts a sensitive
cuckold who refuses to stand up for
himself and shares emotions
with others.

They altered the bodies of women to sell
more copies of their magazine.

—Because women with altered bodies develop

an insatiable need to read.

Something that a lot of men do not
do currently is placing a priority
on nurturing individuals above the
authoritative figures with power over
women. Those comfortable with sitting
at the head of the table are rarely
challenged to sit amongst those who
beg for scraps at their feet, as the
temporary mask of their innermost
insecurities subside to reveal a
dominant male figure who is capable of
controlling his environment for even a
moment.

This older ad is figuratively saying, men are gross and slobs and if you have a harry back women won't like you.

Unfortunately for Gillette and this study, the ad did not immediately reach its goal to change all stereotypes of masculinity.

What happened to those average 13-years-old girls that do not think about being labeled to match up to society standards because of specific measures of being labeled?

Male-induced terror and female fear are not new entertainment concepts that ended in 1996 or began near the turn of the century.

—*1996 was pretty pivotal.*

Georgia uses her beauty and sexiness
like a gun that can never run out
of bullets.

Being a widow is more acceptable than being a divorcee, but both of those are better than the woman who married out of wedlock.

If we deny male survivors their spotlight or their right to simply be victims, then we allow altruism to fester and grow.

—And that cannot be allowed.

She was sexually harassed or grouped every day.

Avoid condensation when addressing
the victim of sexual harassment.

—Things can get so misty.

Fractured History

When you don't look historical facts up and just wing it based on what you think you overheard your grand-father saying at the kitchen table one night when you were 4 years old.

White people were to blame from the 90s on.

—*There. That's settled.*

To begin with the racial system in the U.S., we already know that there is a lot of segregation in the U.S., where each area consists of the most populated race, and racial segregation has been in the U.S. decades ago and still happens up until now.

Though she is not a millennial, Ida B. Wells arguably was at the forefront of some of the civil rights issues that are still being hashed out to this day.

—Had she only been a millennial, maybe there wouldn't have been an argument.

Through this assignment, I learned a bit about how different kids have it today growing up with TV and devices with streaming capabilities compared to the 19th century.

> —*You know, that century with all the years starting with "19—."*

We get to hear what is said behind the curtain and watch them ask the questions about sex, religion, masturbation, etc. All subjects that were never to be discussed outside of the drawing room.

—*Apparently, drawing room conversations were once much livelier than typically imagined.*

Destructive segregations amongst the White American and Black African American communities occurred nationwide during the 1960s, famously known as the Civil Rights Movement.

The Korean War was an interesting part of history, for all nations that participated.

—*A cheery take.*

"Netflix vs. the World" is a
heartwarming story about how Netflix
went from just being a small company
in Silicon Valley to being a media giant.

> —*If you are a corporation in need of*
> *a heartwarming story.*

The speech that addressed the nation
following the Pearl Harbor attack by
Japan has, and hopefully will, "live in
infamy." President Roosevelt's speech
utilized impeccable word choice,
situational severity, tempo, as well
as other techniques which ultimately
allowed him to control and maintain
silence through this historic moment.

—*FDR's famously soundless rhetoric.*

After talking with my mom, I realized
that life before cable and streaming TV
was very simple.

For decades, TV has controlled the flow of information in our universe.

—*Uh-oh. Tell Mars.*

Elvis Presley's death was as devastating as a natural disaster would seem.

He denounced himself as neither black or white, but rather he was simply OJ Simpson.

In the popular press it was stated how journalism is not the way it is today.

According to our PowerPoint lecture, the term "couch potato" became more common for my grandma's family.

It follows a group of girls and one of
their male cousins as they go through
life in the boring planes of Ireland.

—Aer Lingus has a lot to answer for.

In fact, the presence of sports existed
before the inception of television.

History may have changed a bit over
the centuries.

American culture is pushed onto other people and this country which was once a melting pot is now a bland broth to which we call soup.

When Logic— and Math— Fail You

Writing clearly requires thinking clearly. So when the thinking bit gets a bit foggy...

I have 3 siblings, of which I am the second youngest.

The dead sit cacophonously motionless.

Lew Wasserman is considered one of
the first Hollywood moguls.

—*Title of paper: "The Last Mogul."*

I believe that it is within the brightest
minds that truth can simply be found
if one reflects even for a moment upon
the brilliance of their thoughts.

An interesting statistic that stood out to me was that 90% of men are the ones that commit murder.

Viewers hold more power than they
think when it comes to the remote.

His face is cringed with his eyes
piercing the man.

—I'd cringe, too, if my eyes were weaponized.

In the face of accusations of the company's efficiency, some call the message hypocritical.

—*Competence is not only annoying, but duplicitous.*

Keeping an objective attitude while reading all sorts of social and cultural media is an important part of creating your own bias.

The demographics of Forbes show that
31.4% of the readers are homes
with kids.

Regardless of the outcome, media still has the power to convince its audience of many things that the audience may or may not be aware of.

—*It's insidious, really.*

Without knowledge comes a sense of vulnerability to the hostility that isn't warranted.

Every country has many flaws, and we need to showcase them to the world, show the beautiful things, and hide the things that are not good but show both sides of the country.

Being there for different communities
can help us lean on one another with
any unjustified issues.

When regarding the world and its issues, people that live in the United States tend to disregard any boundaries that go beyond our soil.

These ideologies can leak into their writing and feed into the public's desire to read what they want to hear.

It is showing an older woman (in her mid-30s or so) as she represents the target market.

—*Apparently, he did not want an A.*

We're doing a study that involves putting a new product in a customer's face for a limited time.

—As long as you don't leave it there.

It appeared as though the Pagans,
Christians, and Jews took their unity in
Christ and used it to fuel their division.

I like to consider the simple
circumference of humans on Earth.

—Body positivity is becoming more global, clearly.

There were 3 major national networks including ABC, NBC, CBS, and PBS.

I used my closest friends for this
assignment and all but one of them is
black. The other is a white woman.

Female sports journalists make up just
11% of women in sports, while men
cover 89%.

Sports Illustrated's collective audience consists of 30 million people; approximately 23 of which are American.

With the beginning of last year concluding the end of 2020, the US has fallen so much because of the justice system and the racial system.

Sports are televised so often,
daily, minutely.

Say That Again?

It's like getting song lyrics wrong. You use a phrase for years and think you know it—but the first time you write it down, it can squirt out sideways.

I had an outer body experience.

Ideas seem to fall by the waste side.

Keeping Johnny Depp's sanity in tact is challenging.

Killing me will make me stronger.

Syria, North Korea, and Iran are the
Excess of Evil.

Sometimes sports fans can become over-enthusiastic. This can sometimes result in back sportsmanship.

Let God take the stirring wheel.

He is the character who experiences
the loss of innocents.

I think it was worthed.

Had this been some new journalist right off the chopping block, they would have been fired the minute this scandal started.

Our first day was working in groups and
answering in-prompted due questions.

Sometimes our paths get foggy and our judgment gets clouted.

He was in dire strains.

This is a short-sided representation.

One of the most gut-retching jobs in the United States is President.

While it's easy to grunt and grown, I
knew it was good for me.

This became blaringly obvious to me.

She fears he'll sub come to the pressure
on the street and end up in jail like his
dad and brothers.

All my feelings were normal and
to be suspected.

She could have presented a much more powerful, mind-bobbling story to reveal the power behind technology and the fact that sooner or later it will have access to our thoughts.

The men just stand there and the women are going to faun all over them.

The movie will definitely take
home a swath of awards for the
cinematography, but otherwise, it will
be a blimp on the radar despite the
all-star cast.

The sounds escalate as the lights come up to reveal a breathless middle-aged couple resting after the throws of passion.

—*It can get like that.*

I am someone who is fascinated with space and just how unfashionably large the area outside of our Earth is.

—I hate that Universe-shaming attitude.

10

Whiplash

*When your sentence starts out heading left and then
suddenly takes a sharp right turn.*

Never let the other guy see you sweat no matter how much it hurts.

At times I drifted off course from
blindfolding myself.

My speech is one that my head football coach gave to our team before the state quarter-finals my senior year of high school that lasted about 10 minutes.

—*That senior year goes by fast.*

Goosebumps littered my arms.

Media stigma, particularly in television
and film, pushes masculinity and
ideas of what is "masculine" so much
so that getting help can be seen as a
weakness in men, while simultaneously
alcoholism runs far more rampant in
men than in women.

Her constant misplacement of words had guests sitting on her every word.

I picture the media as an umbrella that splits into categories.

Hearing every breath and every vocal chord firing off like a gun in the Wild West is extraordinary.

I must emphasize the hence in the
latter part of that sentence.

His facial suggestions also match his standoffish pose.

His smile was sweet and gentle but currently wore a confused frown.

The media swarmed around Clark's haircut.

The saying, "two parts equal a whole,"
plays a part in this significantly.

I dealt with customers on the floor
which helped me develop the ability to
think on my feet.

Two boats landed on the shorelines of Mumbai and ventured through the city with guns, killing 174 people and injuring 239 others.

The personalities of Sports Illustrated fascinate me, never a day goes by when I haven't at least picked one up.

When with friends, the media viewed sparked conversations about sex and relationships.

I'm definitely a curious girl with
a tendency towards good-natured
inquisition; but skilled journalism takes
a lot of gusto.

Volunteering at a homeless shelter or helping out at your local library—these things are small acts of kindness and I think that this is the way we contribute a small grain of sadness to the mountain of dirt.

Even the saltless sidewalks, which did
not anticipate snowfall in the middle of
November, are iced over.

—*When inanimate objects do things.*

If he didn't commit the murder, the blood samples and shoe wouldn't have wanted to be thrown out so badly.

—*When inanimate objects do illegal things.*

11

Oh, You're Not That Bad...

When writing resumes and cover letters for that first job, it's tough to strike a balance between accuracy and confession.

I am a hungry, adequate applicant who would love to work on the marketing team.

I am a senior customer service manager with adverse experience in communication and public relations.

During my career, I will most likely
be in a position where I will be getting
fired, so I think it is important to know
how to effectively communicate.

Getting practice with communication methods of all kinds has helped me find some guidelines that I can take with me as I enter the working class.

As a nanny, I handled stressful situations with children such as allergic reactions and drowning.

I am a sponge who is eager to soak up
knowledge about the logistics industry.

I am a 20-year-old marketing major aspiring to become an essential piece at a successful marketing agency.

12

Weird but Possibly Wise

Even when the grammar is tortured and the sentence structure twisted, there might be a bit of savvy acumen tucked in amongst the syllables.

A leader needs to be confident. They cannot just mumble.

The issue of white privilege is its ability
to distort opinions with a mask of
strength.

Working with men taught her how to laugh off the little things.

I humbly ask you to not bring in any
food or beverages, for these items can
be extremely distracting and harmful if
not handled properly.

Our society has been so caught up with worrying about what others think about each other, when in reality no one even cares.

Let me know how you can help.

The media simply makes people
go crazy.

White people are so focused on themselves when looking into racism, that we fail to look toward our minority peers in order to conjugally resolve the issue.

—*Finally, a solution to the race problem.*

Whether you are screwed left or right,
the President is a controversial topic.

I personally do not have a preference where I receive my information from because I partake in confirmation bias, I attune the information I am receiving to fit my prior beliefs and opinions.

The program broke down barriers on how class and sexuality is portrayed on television and did it in such a way that no one really noticed.

13

I Think They Like Me...

When students evaluate their courses and professors, they don't always know what they are revealing. Or do they?

As Dr. Nettleton harped on in her lecture, Americans aren't the center of attention in media, and we should be used to adapting to things not being up to par for us.

Dr. Nettleton, I thank you for the work that was, for the most part, put into the course.

—*I guess I did take the odd Saturday off now and then.*

I have also appreciated Dr. Nettleton's rousing discussion prompts that have allowed me, and others, to voice our opinions while also considering what are opinion even is to begin with.

—*Or what a homophone is, as well.*

I loved the content that Dr. Nettleton mostly discussed in the lecture, pretty contrary to popular belief.

People believe that just because we live
in the United States we are free, but it is
clear that after Dr. Nettleton's lecture,
this is not the case.

—*I am powerful, indeed.*

In Professor Nettleton's PowerPoint lecture, she accumulates how television has reshifted our culture.

—I do. I have it all right here in a paper bag.

Dr. Nettleton also uses humor quite frequently to break up her long explanations and boring research.

                —*I'm putting this one on my gravestone.*

Although I was afraid of Dr. Nettleton,
I utilized techniques to ease this stress
by praying to Christ before I walked
into her classroom.

I loved how Professor Nettleton did not care what came out of her mouth.

—*Why, thank you.*

14

Afterword

I tell my students, "You don't have to write like a god—you just have to be clear."

If these oversights, bloopers, and misusages inspire you to reach for more coherence on the page—or if you're heading off to college yourself—here are time-honored and utterly essential guides to expressing your smart ideas with the clarity and specificity they deserve.

The Elements of Style
William Strunk, Jr. and E.B. White (yes, that E.B. White)
Every professional writer I know has a dog-eared, duct-taped, battered copy of this on their desk. It is not littered with lots of grammar-tech; it is filled with practical examples. This little book is sinfully cheap and absolutely the most useful thing you'll ever buy, next to proper rainboots. It's also available free online through Gutenberg.org.

The Associated Press Stylebook
http://apstylebook.com
Buy the latest edition, or even a fairly recent one, and hold the answers to all your writing questions right there in your hand. Traditionalists like the spiral-bound version we can scribble in, but there are handy online and social media versions, too.

The Chicago Manual of Style

https://www.chicagomanualofstyle.org/home.html

The University of Chicago Press produces this authoritative, world-wide guide to punctuation, capitalization, sentence structure, academic writing styles, formatting, and elements of clear writing. Buy it online or hard copy, but know it.

The Purdue Online Writing Lab

https://owl.purdue.edu/site_map.html

Purdue University continues to broaden and deepen this excellent reference for popular and academic writers, students and professors, amateurs and pros. All academic styles are covered, as well as sections on writer's block, drafting applications for university and grad school, the structure of a school paper, and more and more and more. Each time I visit I am newly impressed, and I require my students to visit this site often of a semester.

About the Author

Pamela Hill Nettleton is an award-winning academic, writer, and editor. Twenty-three of her books are in publication—including a biography of Shakespeare and three series of children's books. More than 300 of her essays and features have appeared in magazines, newspapers, and websites; her books and research have been cited in *HuffPost.com*, *The New York Times*, *USA Today*, *Washington Post*, and *Ask Amy*. She teaches at two universities in the Midwest and her academic research focuses on domestic violence coverage in media. Visit her website at PamelaHillNettleton. com

About the Illustrator

Kevin Cannon is an award-winning cartoonist and illustrator whose cartoon maps have appeared in books and newspapers around the world. He may be best known for illustrating and co-writing the critically acclaimed *Cartoon Introduction to Philosophy* (Hill & Wang, 2015). Cannon lives in Minneapolis with his wife Maggie and son Ulysses.

About the Publisher

The Sager Group was founded in 1984. In 2012 it was chartered as a multimedia content brand, with the intent of empowering those who create art—an umbrella beneath which makers can pursue, and profit from, their craft directly, without gatekeepers. TSG publishes books; ministers to artists and provides modest grants; and produces documentary, feature, and commercial films. By harnessing the means of production, The Sager Group helps artists help themselves. For more information, please see www.TheSagerGroup.net.

More Books from The Sager Group

So You Wanna Be a Teacher: A Memoir
by Peter Kravitz

*The Deadliest Man Alive: Count Dante, The Mob
and the War for American Martial Arts*
By Benji Feldheim

The Detective and Other True Stories
by Walt Harrington

Meeting Mozart: A Novel Drawn from the Secret Diaries of Lorenzo Da Ponte
by Howard Jay Smith

Death Came Swiftly: A Novel About the Tay Bridge Disaster of 1879
by Bill Abrams

A Boy and His Dog in Hell: And Other Stories
by Mike Sager

*The Stories We Tell: Classic True Tales
by America's Greatest Women Journalists*
by Patsy Sims

Lifeboat No. 8: Surviving the Titanic
by Elizabeth Kaye

Hunting Marlon Brando: A True Story
by Mike Sager

See our entire library at TheSagerGroup.net

Artifex Te Adiuva

CPSIA information can be obtained
at www.ICGtesting.com
Printed in the USA
BVHW040605300722
643397BV00002B/109